Robert Dockery's
Survival Guide
For
Autistic
People

Robert Dockery's
Survival
Guide
For
Autistic
People

ASA Publishing Corporation
25 S. Monroe St., Monroe, Michigan 48161
An Accredited Publishing House with the BBB
www.asapublishingcorporation.com

All Rights Reserved. No part of this publication may be reproduced, stored in a retrieval system or transmitted in any form or by any means electronic, mechanical, photocopying, recording or otherwise, without the prior written permission of the publisher. Author/writer rights to "Freedom of Speech" protected by and with the "1st Amendment" of the Constitution of the United States of America. This is a work of non-fiction; an autobiographic survival learning guide. Any resemblance to actual events, locales, person living or deceased that is not related to the author's literacy is entirely coincidental.

With this title/copyrights page, the reader is notified that the publisher does not assume, and expressly disclaims any obligation to obtain and/or include any other information other than that provided by the author except with permission. Any belief system, promotional motivations, including but not limited to the use of non-fictional/fictional characters and/or characteristics of this book, are within the boundaries of the author's own creativity in order to reflect the nature and concept of the book.

Any and all vending sales and distribution not permitted without full book cover and this copyrights page.

Copyrights©2023, Robert Lee Dockery, All Rights Reserved
Book Title: Robert Dockery's Survival Guide For Autistic People
Date Published: 04.23.2023
Book ID: ASAPCID2380863
Edition: 1 *Trade Paperback*
ISBN: 978-1-960104-08-3
Library of Congress Cataloging-in-Publication Data

This book was published in the United States of America.
Great State of Michigan

INTRODUCTION

I just wanted to introduce myself to the world. I am not just another autistic male, but I am just Robert Dockery.

"I am just like everybody else. I take it day by day and don't make excuses."

I just want to be a voice for "The Autism Community," and if I can do it, I know then you can do it too.

Robert Dockery's Survival Guide for Autistic People

ACKNOWLEDGEMENTS

I was always

supported with my disability by

Mom, Siblings, Family, Teachers, Friends, and

Coworkers

What is Autism or Autism Spectrum Disorder?

Autism or Autism Spectrum Disorder is a developmental disorder of variable severity that is characterized by difficulty in social interaction, communication, and by restricted or repetitive patterns, or thoughts and behavior.

People with Autism may behave, communicate, interact, and learn in ways that are different from most other people. Autism can present many different challenges depending on the person with autism.

I view autism as an opportunity to be more open about yourself. And I view autism as a different way of seeing the world.

My book is about my upbringing with autism. As a child and the challenge, I was presented with early on and I overcame them.

I have some ideas that I would like to share with you because this is just an introduction of who I am. Here are some of my ideas such as my special connections with sports and music.

The cover explains my journey and its very intentions to the point.

Table of Contents

Introduction 1

Acknowledgements 3

What is Autism or Autism Spectrum Disorder? 5

Chapter 1

Bullying 11

Chapter 2

My Work Experiences 29

Chapter 3

Intervention 67

Chapter 4

Socialization 71

Chapter 5

Academics 79

My Ideas For My Next Books 83

Robert Dockery's
Survival
Guide
For
Autistic
People

CHAPTER ONE

Bullying

My experience with bullying started when I was growing up as a child in and out of school, and outside the home. One of the things that I would experience at school was the kids would always make jokes about how I would read aloud to the class like you do. Read aloud to the class, or they would be like shut up already. This would hurt my feelings because at the time, I could not help myself reading out loud to myself as this helped me understand the books that I was reading at the time a lot better.

Also, the kids in my class would say things like, "Not this guy again."

I would tell them, "I like to read out loud to myself because this helps me learn better."

And they would be, "Can you just read in the hallway?" in a mean way.

I just dealt with it because I did not want the kids to label me as a snitch, or did not want to fight, to get a suspension. So, I just dealt with the punches as they came.

Another thing that I would deal with in school. Is when I had team sports/gym class. The gym teachers at the time would put me on the competitive team. I on the other hand was not very good at sports. So, when I was playing with my competitive teammates, they would say mean things to me like, "Bro catch the ball," in a mean way, if we were playing football.

If we were playing basketball if I had missed

a shot or did not rebound the ball, they would say things like, "Bro don't come to school tomorrow," or they would say, "Bro you not getting the ball no more."

This made me really mad, and I would just ignore them. And tell myself that they not gonna be nothing ten years from now, or I would tell myself I'm letting God handle them.

I also would tell my mom and my sister Katrina the things that they had said at the time. And they would tell me, "You need to start sticking up for yourself." Because at the time I had a tendency to ignore things. And not responding back with them, or I would just blow it off. And did not tell them because I wanted to handle things on my own.

And this would make my sister Katrina upset that I would blow things over and not tell them, and she would say things like, "Don't be scared to tell your family things that happened to you because we are here to help you."

And from that point forward when she had told me that, I would tell my family things that happened to me. And my family was a great support system when it came to bullies, at school. They would give me the strength that I need to go to school the next day at the time.

Also, my competitive teammates would yell at me and the other autistic people that were on my team at the time. They would have my other autistic teammates at the time who were better than me at sports say mean things to me, because I was not good at sports. And because my other Autistic teammates at the time were on the lower end of the Autism Spectrum. They would try to have them say other things like, "You can't shoot, or you suck at basketball."

But my other autistic teammates did not like what they had been doing. So, they told one of their friends, and their friend would be a great support system to help them get over the bullying, which was going on at the time.

Also, if we were playing Hockey, the competitive teammates would put me in roles that they knew I was not good in. For example, I was not a good goalie, and I would tell them like, "I am not good at playing goalie." And they would be like, but you got to play goalie, or they would force me to play goalie. So, they could make fun of me, because they knew that I wasn't good at playing goalie. And how I handled this was I just went along with it, because I did not want to get a bad grade for that day.

I remember telling my family that I wanted to switch to a different team. At the time because of the bullying that was going on at the time. And at the time this was starting to take a toll on me mentally. As I would think about the things that they had said to me a lot. And my family told me. "That, you do not need to switch teams, you need to stick up for yourself, and tell them "You to leave you alone." And as a result, I would have had some good days in team sports/gym at the time, but the bullying still was happening to no avail. So, I just had to go through it to graduate from High school.

Also, I remember an incident back in 2016. When I had looked at a girl and she looked back at me, and she asked me, "Bro are you retarded or something."

And after she asked me that, I told my sister Katrina about it, and she said that we are about to find her and confront her about what she said. But we could not find her.

I also remember feeling hurt that she would say and assume that about someone, that she did not know. And I just ignored her and went about my day in school.

I also got bullied outside of school too, and the people who would bully me would say mean things to me like, "You are retarded." Or they would have short initials for me, "L.D." which means, "Learning Disability," and they would call me that. And that would make me snap back at them, or it would make me really sad that they would call me those names.

My family would go and confront these people and even fight them because they were so mean to me. And as a result, some of them had stopped messing with me completely, and then some just continued to bug me.

For example, I remember I had just moved into my new house back in 2011. I met this guy who had a burn mark on his temple, and I also met two other guys that were with him. We happened to be over on the porch, at the time and were talking, and getting to know each other. As I was the new guy on the block at the time Next thing you know, the guy who had the burn mark on his temple went and pushed me off the porch and my lip was bleeding.

I went home crying telling my family and my

brothers at the time, Darnell and Denzell. They were mad and they wanted to beat the crap out of him. But my mom was like he is a kid, and you cannot do that. And this would be a kid that I would have a problem with from 2011-2014. He would have problems with everybody on the block, and not just me. He would go around breaking things, and he would get in trouble with other people on the block because he was so destructive, and so mean to the other kids on the block.

How I handled him was, if he were to mess with me, I would fight him because my family would tell me that I had to. And I did because he would push me to my limits, tease and belittle me. I would just fight him because of that, and I would win the fights. Because I had stood up for myself.

My family would eventually get into it with his family, back in 2013. The reason we got into it with his family was that he was starting drama with us and other people. His sister at the time, Nana, had said, "Scum out the way," to my sister. And also, his cousins at the time had said, "Scum out of the way," to my sister also.

My sister, like me, got somebody for you and the next thing you know, my brother had ran up in his house trying to fight one of his cousins or whatever. But his cousins were scared and ran back into the house.

I also remember when I used to go to the Recreation Center back in 2010 and 2011 for summer day camp. And when I got there some kids there would invade my privacy. When I would get changed in one of the locker rooms. And they would say things like "You got a small private part," or they would point to it. When they would see me change in the locker rooms to go swimming.

I remember on my way to the swimming pool I would see a puddle of pee on my way going to the pool. I thought at the time that the nasty man and I had felt so uncomfortable on my way going to the swimming pool. Also, when I would get done swimming, I would be scared to go back to the locker room to go change. Because of the Kids that were looking at me at the time. So, what I would do was wait until most of the kids were gone, and then I would go back into the locker room to go change so the kids would not be looking at me.

I also remember some little boys would pick on me and tease me for having a little privacy and how I handled that was I would tell them things like, "Don't worry about what the size of my private was," or my sister would stick up for me and tell them like, "Don't worry about it." Or she would encourage me to stick up for myself against the boys.

The little boys that would pick on me would call me things like, "Ali" and I would tell them, "My name is not Ali." And that my name was "Robert or Buddy." But they would just call me "Ali," only and at that, I did not know why they did it.

As a result of the bullying that was going on this caused me to want to fight more often if I had started to defend myself more against the little boy that picked on me because the bullying would become too much for me.

For example, this one little boy started to pick on me and I started to lose it. Suddenly, I snapped and beat the little boy up that was messing with me.

And I got in trouble by one of the staff members who was working at the Recreation Center at the time told me that I had to go home for the day. And I was mad because I'm like, "He started with me first."

And one of the staff members was like, "I don't care you got to go home."

So, I was like, "I'll go home."

There was another time when a little kid had started something with me, and I again snapped and hit him.

Another staff member during that time told me, "That the little kid is a baby, and since you are older you could have hurt him."

I learned a very valuable lesson that day, you got to control your anger around people, and from that point forward I did just that.

I remember one day I also had to come home from school and some guys across the street from my granny's house had water balloons and the next thing you know they had started throwing water balloons at me. They kept it going.

I told them, "That I would go tell my dad what they had done." And my dad did nothing as I told him what had happened. Since his car was wet. And I felt so sad that my dad did not help me, with the guys that were throwing water balloons at me and got his car wet. I just dealt with it, just as my dad told me, "Don't worry about them," and I did not. I remember getting bullied outside of school back in 2013 when this one girl used to make fun of me for jumping. My sister said, "Don't be making fun of my little brother." She was mad and disrespectful about it. So, my sister fought her because of it.

And one of the neighbors had knocked on my mom's door because they had been fighting on their property.

Mom said, "My daughter had a right to fight her because she had been disrespecting my son." And from that point on it was the end of it.

My advice to autistic people who are dealing with bullying in school and out of school is unless he or she said something really hurtful or put their hands on you then you have a right to defend yourself from the bullying that is happening. Regardless of what a teacher says, someone who is bullying me said for example, "Your mama is broke." And my mama passed away. I would feel some type of way and hit them.

Also, if something is happening to you in school. Don't be afraid to talk to your family member or a close friend about bullying. Because that could help you find solutions to the bullying. As a result, you are going to feel better about what happened at school with bullying.

And based on my experiences with bullying outside of the home I would base my experiences of bullying include your family in everything that happens to you. When it comes down to bullying because they are the ones that are going to, have your back no matter what.

I have made mistakes of trying to handle the bullying on my own outside, at home, or at school by not telling my family. And I would get in trouble with my own family, for not telling them. The bullying would get to me mentally because I held it in for so long.

Also, I would advise that you to stick up for yourself more than I did outside of school. If you don't the bullying will continue because they feel that they don't have to respect you.

Also, if someone is pressuring you to do things that you don't want to do, then don't hang out with this person. Because that person could be a bully in their own way. And these might be jealous of you because of how you may carry yourself, or you might be doing well in life. They want to take you down because they are not doing good themselves. By having you do unhealthy things that they do like smoking and drinking. So that you can become addicted to these things. And you wind up losing everything because of them. So, don't listen to them and stay true to yourself, no matter how weird people think that you are. The right person will accept you for who you are and more.

For non-verbal autistic people, my advice for parents to check on their son or daughter every day before and after school, to see how they are feeling, and check for any scratches or sores that they may have because non-verbal autistic people can't communicate needs or wants. As a result, this may put them at risk for bullying at school or outside of school.

So, this is important for parents to also check other things like a change in behavior, as a result of bullying. For example, your non-verbal autistic is happy most time of the time. But one day he or she might come home crying, or maybe upset. Then you may need to check to see if bullying is going on in the school. That he or she goes to because that might be part of the problem.

I also advise that non-verbal Autistic's parents be active within the school because then as a parent you gain more insight into what goes on in your son or daughter's school that they go to, so you can handle the bullying or anything else. That might go on a little more smoothly and also, I would try to gain more insight into where your non-verbal Autistic son or daughter is coming from, mentally and emotionally. It's the best way that you can since they have a hard time communicating so you can change schools if your son or daughter is constantly feeling depressed as a result of bullying that is going on in their school.

Also, you just have to understand as a non-verbal autistic parent that the bullying might not understand where your non-verbal autistic child is coming from so. You just got to understand the bully's perspective too.

CHAPTER TWO

My Work Experiences

My experiences in the workforce began in the summer of 2018, when I had started to work at a place called Cass Community Center in Downtown Detroit.

When I started to work there, I immediately met some good staff members who would help me be more sociable, and the staff members would also teach me some valuable lessons in life that I still cherish to this day. Because the lessons that they taught me are a big reason why I would later make it far in life to go to trade college and land a very good job.

Also, I met some very good co-workers on the job that I am still very close with still this day.

I would do my job very good and as a result, this would impress the bosses who were at the job at the time, and they would be like one of my bosses, which is only seventeen. I was only seventeen at the time as well. Coming to work and following directions very good at the time, while the rest of them are all older than him and they were just goofing around.

I did janitorial work in a warehouse. My co-workers and I would go back and forth to the warehouse and the Scott buildings to clean the bathrooms. I would do a very good job cleaning the bathrooms and my co-workers also did a very good job. This made me really like the job as we worked as a team. When it came down to doing our work, I had very close bonds with my co-workers. We would talk over our lunch and breaks.

As a result of this, I wanted to come back for next summer. I asked my mom if I could come back, and she said, "Yes," and the next thing you know my mom and my support coordinator, at the time had set me up so I could go back to Cass at the time.

I worked at Cass Community in the summer 2019 but this time I worked as a paper sorter. This was a job where you had to take the colored paper off of the conveyor belt and leave and sort it on a long white sheet. We would be in the warehouse sorting paper most of the time.

When it was time for our lunch, we would eat at the Scott Building. Me and my co-worker would talk during our lunch and breaks.

Me and a fellow staff member who worked at Cass named Mr. Madison would always talk to me about sports. When we were at the warehouse sorting paper, we would develop a close bond with each other as he was like a father figure to me, in lots of ways. With the way that we had socialized at the time.

I had developed a close relationship with a guy named Chuck who was our boss at the time. And he would talk to us about his personal experience. This taught me a lot about life to this day. About how to go about things at the adult level, and this taught me about what things to stay away from.

Also, me and my co-workers at the time would take field trips to go places like Bel Isle, and to the park, and Chuck would buy us pizza from Little Caesars. I would always thank Chuck for what he did for us because no other boss was doing what he did at that time.

And also, when we were sorting paper, he would always tell us to do our work. I would always do a good job of following directions on the job and moving at a quick pace the best that I could do at the time.

I also had socialized with other co-workers

who worked at different positions at Cass Community at the time for example I meet a guy named Sam at the time. Me and Sam just clicked automatically as he shared the same interests as me at the time. Such as playing video games, watching wrestling, basketball, etc. and we would play video games over my house all the time. We had a lot of fun.

I would be close with a co-worker. She and I would socialize about things that happened on the job and stuff that was going on in my life as well. When she and I would sort papers together we would work well together so this was a very good friendship that we had.

Everybody in general would love me on the job because of the way I carried myself and my work ethics on the job. I got a lot of compliments on both of my jobs at Cass from my bosses, and as a result they would always want me to come back on the job.

I would go on to Trade College in the fall of 2021 to be a CNA. But first I had to pass my IQ test to get into Trade College in 2020. I remember I was so scared that I was not going to pass that day that I took it. I remember trying the best that I could on it and the testing lady told me, "Do the best that you can," along with my mom at the time. Next thing you know the testing lady calls my mom while she was on our family vacation Put-In-Bay at the time to tell my mom that I had passed my college IQ test to get in.

The next thing you know my mom calls me and tells me that I passed, and I felt so happy inside that I had passed it. And it was like a huge weight had just been lifted off my shoulders at that time, because I kept on beating myself up.

Thinking my family was not going to be happy with me if I had failed my college IQ test. I had called my brothers, to tell them that I had just passed my college IQ test.

He was so proud of me and said to me, "If I had fifty dollars, I would split it with you, twenty-five dollars is yours. Because I'm so proud of you for doing the thing I did not do."

Next, I had to take some Aptitude tests, on the computer also in 2020 and I had to do good on those to qualify for the trade CNA. At the time I ended up doing really good.

Oh! those instructors who were with me at the time said that I was really dedicated to do what I was doing, that I did a good job, while I was taking my Aptitude tests, Math, and Reading."

I also remember all 2021 up until I left for college. My family and I would talk about the excitement of leaving for college and how proud they were of me.

I remember having to buy the things that I had needed for college and my family was a good help with me getting ready for college and setting up things such as a rental that I needed to take me to Trade College.

I remember the days leading up to me leaving. I was a little bit nervous, and I remember being worried about my family being okay while I was going to college, because I love my family. I had to make sure that my family was ok before I had to go.

On such things like making sure they had someone to talk to, buying things that they need like food or money to go buy other things they want or need.

My family had thrown me a going away party. The day before I had left for college. My Aunt Shirley, Uncle Joe, and Aunt Tina were there to support me while I was going away. My family would come to take pictures of me so that they would have memories of me leaving for college.

And the next day we left for college in the rental we had rented. The whole car ride I still remember was so exciting for me heading off to college. My sister's boyfriend at the time told me stories of how his cousin who was in college at the time, met people and how college life changed him. Also, he would tell me that you had to get the girls in college, don't let the White guys be on anything weird.

We had finally made it after a long car ride. And I got to see my dorm room. My dorm room was nice as I had brought my stuff in with my family helping out.

My room had two bunk beds but due to covid at the time I had to have the room to myself. I was happy because this meant that I had the privacy to do what I wanted to do, at my own will, and this also made me really love my own privacy within myself.

I remember the last moments I would spend with my family before they left. They would take pictures of me, trying to have their last conversations with me about how they wanted me to be safe and study really hard so that I would graduate. From Trade College and get my CNA certificate at the time.

Before my family had left, we would take a tour around the school to see what it was like, and I had found out that my class was close to my dorm room. During the tour I really liked this good thing because I don't have to go a far distance between my dorm and the classroom. And we also went to go see the gym which was big. And we went to go see the swimming pool at the time which was big. My mom was like this is a nice big pool. But due to covid at the time the pool was closed. I was so disappointed at the time because I love swimming. Swimming is a good way for me to calm down and get out some energy.

The next thing you know my family had left and I was by myself in my dorm room feeling kind of nervous thinking about how the teachers were going to be. What was going to be their approach to doing things with me and other students at the time?

The school that I had went to was MCTI Trade College. It is a trade college for autistic students like me. School really helps the students with disabilities find trades that they can excel in and then place them as soon as they graduate from MCTI.

Also, the teachers there are really nice to you, and they will do the best that they can to fill the wants and needs of their Autistic Students that go there.

I remember my first day in class my three instructors were introducing themselves to the class and shared with us the disabilities that they have. This made me relax. Because I myself had some challenges with my disability, as they did.

With things such as paying attention and the school district labeling us as having "Special Needs." Because we learned differently than the rest of the students. And the other students picking on us. Because they don't understand the way that we process things, or the students are just really mean in general.

This also made me really comfortable with the entire flow of the classroom. And this made me really buckle down and study for my test and quizzes. That I would go on to take in the class.

I mainly wanted to make my family proud of me. And also prove to those people who wronged people with a disability. In how we go about things such as school, outside interaction, etc.

I also made really good friends in MCTI that would help me study for tests and quizzes; their names were Amari, Marian Lynn, Luke, and Anya.

I also had a friend named Najee Mro, I would talk to about football and played video games together in my dorm room. Whenever I needed someone to talk to, I would talk to her. She was always there for me, besides studying. She would offer me snacks because she knew that I did not have any unless I bought some in my dorm room at the time.

My other friend Maian-Lim would really be a big help to me as we would study after class so that I could pass my test and quizzes, and when clinics came. (Clinics is when you start working with the resident in an actual nursing home). She would practice with me and Luke after class and we would practice on dumbs at the things that we were supposed to do to pass clinics at the time. I would pass go on to pass clinics and my test and quizzes because of the great help my college friends gave me to eventually graduate MCTI.

I also would go to the gym to exercise whenever I could after school to help keep me focused, to get myself in shape. I had a really good time exercising. It helped me release some energy, to give me a good night's sleep. I would take a shower after I got done exercising. I would eat well because I would save the seconds that I got from lunch and store them in my mini fridge at the time for when I got done from exercising. It helped me set a routine after school to go exercise. My friend Najee and I would also exercise after school, she also wanted to stop first.

I go to the gym to go jog, the weight room to lift weights, and one of the long weights that they had there my friend Jay whom I met my first day at MCTI would come spot me on the weights, and I did good for my first time lifting. I was really proud of myself for doing good because I did not think I could do good at first. But my friend Jay really encouraged me. And I just stuck in there and did it. I also did pushups and ran on the treadmill that they had there. Also, I would do crunches on one of the mats that they had there.

Also, in the clinics, I would work with a resident and Evelyn Dunning, they were nice to the resident to us, and they were willing to listen to my stories that I had to share with them. My instructors at the time were really impressed with me. For finding a way to relate to them and socialize with them. Because to the instructors socializing was very important in connecting and building a relationship with the resident.

For example, I also worked with a guy who likes to watch the television show George Lopez and I connected with him, because I liked that show at the time, and because at the time People who worked with would not understand what he was saying.

At the time, the instructors were really impressed because of what I could do by connecting with him. With something that he liked at the time.

Also, my instructors would be impressed with the way that I felt the residents because I gave them some time to eat, just in case, they were slow eaters or had a restriction at the time. I also did a good job washing the residents. I would go on to pass clinicals because I would do a good job with the residents as well with socialization and doing what the instructors told me to do at the time.

The next thing you know the state test came up and I would study after school for the state test just like we had done for the test, quizzes and clinicals, and we would go over all the things that we had learned all throw out the semester, and I did really well with. This started building my confidence for the state test, like I am going to pass. At that point I had done well all semester with my test and quizzes scoring A's and like one B and just recently at the time clinicals we also studied all of our skills that we learned threw out the semester like making the bed while a resident was in it, emptying a resident urinary bag, and properly transferring a resident from a bed to wheelchair/wheelchair to bed using a gilt belt.

On the day of the state test, I was very confident but also very nervous because of the pressure that was on me at the time to make my family proud of me. Thinking like what if I fail this state test is my family going to be disappointed in me for doing all this for me just to turn around and fail the test and I got a retake it again and possibly fail again.

There walking in the testing room all I remember when I sat down to take the test on the computer reading the questions and just answering the questions the best that I could. I just keep on taking the test on the computer. The next thing you know I was done. I had passed the test part on the computer. I remember just feeling relieved that I had passed because I was reading the questions on the test and I was really confused because of the way that they had worded it, the test at the time. I just answered the questions to the best of my ability at the time.

Next, I had taken my skills part of the state test and the skills that I got was the emptying the urinary bag, transferring a resident from wheelchair to bed doing a hand care, but at first, I had to wash my hands and I did really good at this skill, so I had passed it.

Next, I had done the emptying the urinary bag still and I had introduced myself to the person that you are working with at the time because if you wanted to pass the skills you had to introduce yourself to the person that you are working with to make them comfortable.

Then I told the person that I was working with, "That I was going to get my supplies, then I'll be right back." Because you were also required to tell them the tools needed. if you wanted to pass. I went and got my supplies that I had needed to get. Then I placed a paper towel up under the urinary bag and I put my measuring cup up under the bag. I emptied the urinary bag and told the testing lady the urine measurement at the time, and I poured the urine in the toilet. The next thing I did was clean the measurement cup with water and a paper towel. The next thing I did was take off my gloves washing my hands, but I made sure to do this procedure currently so that the testing lady would not ding me for it, and I told my person that I was working with that I was done with emptying the urinary bag and the testing lady had passed me for the skills.

Next, I had to do the transferring skill and I introduced myself to the person that I was working with. I told the person that I was going to get my supplies and I would come back. The next step I did was get the person up and put the gait belt on the person and use it to transfer the person to the wheelchair, but I had to make sure the wheelchair was locked so that the person would not fall because if the person fell then it would be my fault and the testing lady would ding me. I had transferred my person to the wheelchair using very effective body mechanics so that I would not get hurt and I locked the wheelchair too along with bringing the wheelchair close to the bed so the procedure could be easier for me and the person that I was working with at the time.

The next thing I did was transfer my person from the wheelchair to the bed using the same body mechanics and telling my person what I was going to do before I did it. The next step I did was transferring the person to the bed, then I was going to put away my supplies and come back. And I told the person that I was going to put the call button in reach for the person so that person could reach it. I had done this for both skills at this point because this was also required if I wanted to pass the skills.

I had started to do the hand care skill and I would do the same things introduce myself to the person I was working with and telling them what I was going to do, and getting the supplies that I needed to do the skill and coming back with the supplies/provide privacy with the curtain before I had left to get the supplies for the three skills that I did at the time.

Next, I had begun to do the hand care on my person as I would have my person test the water out first before I just do the care and my person said the water was good. So, I put the person's hand in the water and put soap in the water using a washcloth, and I started washing the person's hand in the water. Next, I would take the person's hand out of the water and place the person's hand on a towel to dry. I would go on to clean my person's nails with an orange stick. I would be very careful with the way that I was cleaning the nails with a file stick, and I would make sure to do it gently, so the person wouldn't get uncomfortable. The next thing you know I put away my supplies and told the person I was working with that I was going to place a call button so that they could reach it. I also provided privacy for myself.

The next thing you know the testing lady had

told me, "That I had passed the skills part of my test. Because I had met the requirements that was expected of me at the time."

And I was so happy that I had passed both the computer and the skills part of my test at this point. And I called my mom, dad, sister, and brother to tell them that I had passed my state test at the time. They were so happy for me.

Also, they were so proud of me for just going up there to college on my own at the time, and really focusing on the things that I needed to focus on. Not letting anybody distract me from getting my work done in college.

When they printed mine, my CNA Certificate at the time, I felt really proud of myself for just going into college.

In a trade that I was not familiar with and finding success. In that trade by passing with A's and one B, because I put in the work to study. I really learned the material at the time and my instructors were really happy with me and my other MCTI classmates for passing the state test at the time.

On the day of my graduation was really nervous but at the same time very excited, because of what I had accomplished. And I was also very excited to see my family because I had not seen them in over two months at this point.

And was doing a video of graduation where the parents could see their kids walking up to them with their CNA certificate in their hand/with their cap and gown on them. I remember I had to stand in line to get in the classroom and the instructors had called me and the students to get in the classroom, we sat in chairs while the instructors were trying to get the parents videos together so that we could see our families. I had my gown and cap on while I was waiting for the parents, video and when the instructors got the parents on. I saw my sister Katrina and her best friend on the video. I was surprised to see on the video, but at the same time really proud of her for supporting me at my graduation at the time.

Next, the instructors called the students up to go see their parents with CNA certificate with their cap and gown on and the other students.

The parents were really proud of them for graduating from Trade College. When my name was called, I had walked up with my certificate in my hand and my mom Katrina, and her friend were proud of me. They were so excited to see me with my certificate and my gown on. I told them that I loved them and that I thank God for having them in my life every single day because they have done so much for me at this point. With their support and my mom pushing me and providing guidance to help me get to this point in my life.

Also, my instructors were so happy for me and the students for getting to this point, and they gave us hugs, and told our parents that we had did a very good job to get to this point."

Next, after graduation, I had went to my dorm room and I thought man I am going to be an inspiration to my family because I was the first in the family to go to college and graduate. On the day when my family came to pick me up from Trade College, they were so proud of me, but also very excited to see me because they hadn't seen me in two months at this point. Also, we were talking about how things were at home, and we were talking about how it was just amazing that I just been the first out of the family to graduate college. I told my family, "That all I mostly did was study and grind in college."

Next, I had my stuff that I had packed up before my family came up to the school. My Family and I put the stuff in the rental car that we were using at this time. When we had all the stuff in the car, we started the road home.

My mom handed me a new phone that she bought me because my phone was broken while I was in college. Next thing I knew we were finally home. I was excited to see my dogs, Mello, and Tobi. They were so happy to see me in the backyard, it was nighttime. They jumped up on me and tried to lick my face because they loved me, and they were wondering like, where have you been?

From that point on I would stay home for a short while. Then my mom started telling me that we should start looking for CNA jobs. But I just wanted to chill out, because at the time I just came home from college. But my mom was like, "NO! You need to get your butt up and try to look for a job." I was like, "Mom . . . OK."

We had gone to a nursing home named Oak Pointe and this was my first-ever job interview. So, I was very nervous, scared, and anxious. But my mom encouraged me to do the best that I could do at the time. So, I could land the job.

The next thing you know I had talked to the person that was interviewing me for the job and the person had really liked me so she said, "That she would call me in a couple of weeks, at the time. But she never called me, and I never got the job.

Next, we went to a nursing home that was up the street from my house. Mom and I told the lady there at the time I was interested in the job. The lady told me to fill out a job application, so I filled out the job application and I turned it in to her. So, she said that they were going to get back with me, but they never did.

I remember this one day in 2021 I happened to look at my email. This guy named John who was the one who placed the students that graduated at MCTI sent me and the email saying, "We are hosting a job fair at the Best Western Hotel." I went to tell my mom about the email at the time. So, she was like I'm about to take you up there to this job fair and see what this is about.

So, when went to Best Western Hotel, I talked to various other people about me getting a job at their nursing home. But they would say that I could not work there in their nursing home, because I needed some experience at the time. Because I was new since I had just got my CNA certificate at the time.

So, all of a sudden, I ran across this guy named John and I went up to John like, "Hello my name is Robert Dockery, and I am interested in looking for a CNA job."

A person from Fox Run was very likable and I was delighted to meet that person and have him look at my brochure to see about Fox Run. He can tell me how he liked it. I looked at the brochure for about a minute and told him that I was interested in working at Fox Run.

He really liked me at the time. So, he told me that he wanted to hire me. He said, "I will call you and let you know what I want you to do at Fox Run."

After the job fair, my mom was really proud of me for doing a good job. At the Job Fair. Because

I was presenting myself very well and I spoke in a very professional manner, which is something that you have to do in job interviews if you want to land a job along with letting your personality show in a positive way. And you have to be very presentable when it comes to looks so that the people who are interviewing you can be impressed with the way that you are handling yourself. I also took my resume with me to the job fair so that the people at the job fair could see it to know that I was valid in a way with my experiences, with working in class and me going to trade college. I made sure to keep my resume very neat so that whoever looked at it would look Professional and very neat to people at the job fair because this is what you have to do if you want to land a job also.

A man had called me back after the Job Fair and he told me that I was going to take some classes in orientation, and then I was going to start my training with the other CNA's that worked at Fox

Run at the time. I took my orientation classes at Fox Run at the time and I did very well with the classes and after that when I would start my journey working with the other aides in early 2022 at Fox Run. The aide that would be training with me would show me things like the use of a Hoyer Lift, changing a resident, how to set up the trays, wrapping the silverware, pinning a call button, getting rid of the Hoyer, pad, using the Hoyer Lift and overall, and how to present yourself with the resident.

I would have some growing pains with Fox Run because the trainers I would work with taught me different ways to approach the job. And I was trying to form my own way of doing the job. But first, this was a difficulty for me, because I told my aide that I was training with the different methods the aids had shown me.

And the aide told me that the other aids did not care about the job but rather they just do it for a check. I take pride in my work, and I think you should do the same. Also, the aide that I was working with taught me to let your work speak for yourself. Because the aide did the same at the time and I was liked ok. Also, the aide would have me make sure the tables were organized meaning that were no extra cups on the table and the aide would have me check the garbage can to make sure there weren't any dirty briefs in there because that would contaminate a whole room.

I would go on to do these things that the aide showed me in training for three months and then I had started to work on my own. When I had started working on my own, I would remember the things that my aide had taught me in training, and as a result, I would do a good job as a CAN aide. Because I took very good care of my residents like I was supposed to and I followed directions on the job, which is what you are supposed to do, I also had very good reviews with the resident family.

But I also had growing pains with my job

because I would have an incident with residents because they either did not ring their call button like they were supposed to, or I did not check my list like I was supposed to by accident. I would also have incidents with my residents because of some of the methods the aid taught me, for example, the aide taught me how to change a resident's brief while standing up with the sit-to-stand, and I had did this method with my resident and my resident had ended up fainting because she could no longer grip the sit to stand by, I tried my best I could wipe up quicker because she just had a bowel movement and it was a lot of poop on them. So, I had to get all of it off of them the best I could with the limited time that I had because my aide would get on me about doing things in a timely manner in training, but another aide told me that timing really did not matter as long as you got the job done.

On such things as feeding a resident and things of that nature.

Wiping the residents. The resident had let go of the sit to stand and she ended up fainting to the floor and me. And the nurse at that time had to help get her up from the floor to the bed and I had to fill out an incident report at the time because that is what I had to do if I had an incident with my residents. So, I filled out the report. At first, I thought I was going to be fired because my resident fell but the nurse told me that I was not going to be fired, I felt better about it, and from then on, I would learn from that incident to do better on my job, so I did.

Based on my experience in the workforce I would advise an autistic person entering the workforce to follow directions on the job. Develop a good reputation on your job. Because that lets the bosses on your job know that you are a good worker. It might potentially lead to you earning a raise in your job. Also, I would advise that you don't let a bad co-worker, who wants to put you down, because they are not happy on their job. Get to you because you have to stay positive and keep doing your job the best that you can. And try to avoid that person as much as you can so you won't get in trouble, for feeding off to their negativity. I would also advice that you do your job the best that you can. And don't try hard to impress people on a job or stress out about a job. Because most of the time people on the job do not care about you. They only care about your ability to do the job and that's it.

I would also advise that you find a job that you really like because if you work a job that you don't like chances are you are going to be stressed out and you are going to be really angry at the fact that you have to go to work and that not a good thing because this leads to stuff like depression, and other mental health issues.

Also, I would advise that you enjoy your life outside of work. Because you are not supposed to live to go to work but work to live. Your life such as food, clothes, and shoes. I also advise any autistic person that has any special interests that can earn you some money. I advise that you go take advantage of that because your special talents and special interest might take you very far in many ways, and it might lead to you being able to do more with your family or for yourself, including and possibly move you or your family into a nice home in a new state. It might also make you happy and have an improvement on your mental health, because you used your special talent to do something that you really enjoy.

Instead of sticking at a job where you were unhappy at for eight or more hours a day. For example, when I was working at Fox Run, I happened to go through some growing pains with a co-worker who would yell at me, when they were training me. This would really stress me out at the time because I was trying to kind a form my own patterns of how to do the job, based on what the different trainers told me. The co-worker would tell me things like you need to not take things so personal all the time. But at the time I was thinking you can't expect me not to take things personal. When you are yelling at me and I'm trying my best to do the job.

I remember I would be thinking about them yelling at me about being organized even when they were not even there. And I remember one day when I forgot the call button hooked around the wheelchair and when I was done with hooking the resident up in the Hoyer lift.

My co-worker would notice it and rip me apart. The reason I forgot was I was so busy thinking about her yelling at me. And I was on eggshells thinking what's she going to yell at me about now.

As a result of all of this it made me want to use my special talents and interests to earn some money, instead of staying at Fox Run.

So, I told my mom that I wanted to get into

gaming because I heard that now days gamers could make a lot of money. And mom said, "I am going to see what I can do for you." We looked up gamer's sites and things like that and it was to no avail and the gamers' venture never worked out for me.

I continued to work a Fox Run with my co-worker and I would just deal with my co-worker, and I would just deal with my co-worker until better opportunities came for me to become my own boss. And I'm still doing so as of November 2022.

So, one day when my mom was taking me to work. I said, "I want to write a book about my disability, to inspire people with autism." And my mom had ended up finding a publisher for me and I was so happy because this meant that I could use my special talent to get rich if my book does well to help myself and my family.

So, at the time, I was very excited and so was my family. It had taken so much out of me to want to be an author, but I had found that if I wanted to be my own boss, this was the move I had to make. To get uncomfortable and use this special talent to make myself happy.

I would recommend MCTI for Autistic people looking to go to trade college because the teachers there really work with you, and the school is built to deal with people who have disabilities. Also, MCTI has really good people there that will help you succeed, in the classroom and outside of the classroom as well.

I would also advise parents of Autistic people to have their son or daughter go to MTCI because they have a lot of activities there that can help your autism be more special and excel in trades that fit them to earn a job. The school is called MCTI Institution.

CHAPTER THREE

Intervention

I WOULD ADVISE Autistic Parents to check your son or daughter to see if they are behind in developmental milestones, like walking speaking, crawling, repetitive movements, like hand flapping, or lining things up in a particular order.

Also, if you feel like something off in your gut stick with that gut feeling. Because it is likely that something is wrong with your son or daughter, and you may have to take him or her to a doctor for an autism test. Then, see if the test comes back positive.

Then I would advise that you take him or her to a preschool so that they can work with them because the earlier you put them in school the better chance that they have to be successful later on in life. And they can make really good progress with their autism if you also practice routine. With what the school is doing with them, for example if your preschool is working with your autistic son or daughter with reading then as a parent you should be reading to your son or daughter at home too. So, that you can keep it consistence. Routine that helps your child learn.

Also, I would advise the parents to have your son or daughter point to their colors in books or objects and if your autistic son or daughter points to the correct color then I would advise you congratulate them. Because this means that they are doing what they are supposed to do. And that means that they are learning.

If your autistic son or daughter comes up to

you and grabs you by the hand that means that might want you to do something, or they might want you to interact with them. So, don't get frustrated if they do, this a lot because this is how they communicate, since they are non-verbal.

Also, I preach that the autistic parents be a patient with your autistic child might throw tantrums or screams at top often their voice because they don't know how to communicate yet and they might be around other kids because they like to do their reserved interests. But if you get them around other kids early then they can become more socialized with other kids.

Autism can be hard to detect because autism is present differently in kids so I advise that you pay attention the best way that you can and if your child is showing signs of autism early in life or later in life get them some help.

Regardless, because any intervention is helpful to your autistic child whether it's early or late. But I mostly recommend that it's early because the early it is the better chances your autistic child has to succeed later on in life.

CHAPTER FOUR

Socialization

I would recommend that parents of autistic children try to get their kids to be as social as they can. Because socialization helps them connect with people in the real world.

Also, I would advise that you try to get your son and daughter into sports, because this can help them form new interests and hobbies. That they may enjoy, and this can improve their socialization helps them make new friends in school or outside of school.

For example, when I was coming up as an autistic child myself my mom would introduce me to wrestling. And the wrestling I would watch was called WWE Smack Down at the time, and it came on my TV 20 back in late 2009. The wrestler who would come on the show would go on to have really great matches with each other and their names were Rey Mysterio, CM Punk, Batista, and the Hart Dynasty (David Hart Smith, and Tyson Kidd were their names, and they were a tag team). John Morrison, Drew McIntyre, Eric Escobar, Matt Hardy, Undertaker, Kane, etc. When I watched these guys, it helped me form a new interest as an autistic child. And I was hooked on the tv as soon as the wrestling came on and the storying lines and characters taught me some very important life lessons that I still cherish till this day.

For example, I remember back in 2010 I had watched CM Punk and his group called the Straight Edge Society, on Smack Down and they would always talk about not doing drugs and living a clean lifestyle.

As an autistic, I really took to this and said to myself that I am not going to smoke and drink, and I would look on the back of the cigarette packages and they said that Surgeons do not recommend that you smoke these because TMS causes cancer, and this also inspired me to not smoke or drink.

I also remember back in 2009-2010, when fellow female wrestlers named Mickie James and Michelle McCool would go at it in a storyline that involved Mickie getting bullied. And as an autistic I felt bad for Mickie because Michelle would always bully her and call her names like, "Piggy James," along with Michelle McCool thinking that she was better than everybody at time with her friend Layla McCool.

This inspired me not to bully people and treat people how I want to be treated. I would advise Parents of autistic children based on my experiences also watches sports because sports can also teach them life lessons that they need to thrive in life and lead healthy lifestyles and sports also helps them socialize with other non- autistic people. With similar interest as them for example When I played football with my friends. I had a good time with them because playing football was something me and my friends had in common and also, I played track back in 2017 because I wanted to try something new, and my mom had convenience me to try something new. So, I tried Track & Field. I had ended up really enjoying this type of sport, even though I was bad at it. But I was proud of myself for trying something new that I was not used to.

I would advise that parents encourage their autistic child to keep playing sports because sports help them focus better in school and as a result your child might get better grades in school.

Also, if your autistic child has aggression problems. I would advise that they playa sport like football or boxing because that helps them let go of all that penned up anger that was built inside of them and it helps them channel that aggressiveness on something positive that could help them out in long run to be a boxer or football player and they could make really good money being in the NFL or bring in the boxing leagues.

    I would also advise for parents to get the autistic child of yours to socialize with their family member too because this help them build a long-lasting relationship with their family and this helps the mat when it comes to things like depression and other mental health issues that they may have going on with them mentally because they have a reliable person that they can talk to and not feel Judged when talking to them. For non-verbal autistic people I would advise the parents to play catch with them with a football or a tennis ball. Because this helps you as a parent better connect with your non-verbal son or daughter.

And I would recommend that you take them to swimming pools. Because non-verbal autistic people love being in water because it calms them down and it helps relax them overall. Also, swimming pools help them get out some energy in a positive way and you as the parent are going to have everlasting memories spending time with your non-verbal son or daughter.

I also advise that you take them to parks, movies, etc. because if you take them places, even though they might not be able to talk, they can, however, enjoy themselves. Doing things like swinging on the swings to get out some aggression or they might enjoy watching a movie that is on at the theater.

Also taking them places makes them feel like a regular person in society. Just like everyone else, and as a result you are going to have a happy and healthy non-verbal autistic son or daughter.

I also advise parents of high functional

Autistic people to also take their son or daughter out in the public and take them to places like the movies, swimming pool, parks, etc. because this helps them also be social and form new friends in new places.

Also, this helps them to see what everyday life is like. And it allows them to see life from a different perspective from what they were used to.

CHAPTER FIVE

Academics

I would advise any Autistic person who are currently in school to ask for help if you are struggling in a specific subject such as math, or science because this helps you succeed in school as it allows for you to gain more knowledge and depth about the subject. That you were struggling with. Also, with the teachers' help you could potentially overcome your struggles in school, and you can become good at subjects that you once struggled in and as a result you are going to feel proud of yourself. Because you put in the hard work along with asking for guidance from teachers.

I also would advise any autistic person not to let any teachers make you feel ashamed for learning differently from the rest of the kids in school. Because if you let this get to you this may lead to other mental health problems such as depression or anxiety because the pressure that you might be facing from being different from everybody else might be too much to overcome.

So, I would advise that you be strong and confident in being different.

I would advise teachers to be more flexible when it comes to special needs students because they don't learn the same way as non-special needs students. Because what may be common sense to ever body else might not be common sense to a special need student.

I do advise that teachers not be so impatient with special needs students because they do things in their own way and they learn things at their own pace, whether it's fast or slow.

And also, special needs students have interest that they need to have in order to function throughout their day. For example, they might need to have a special toy, or they might have a book that they are interested in etc.

So, I would advise teachers to create a time where that specific special needs student can enjoy that special toy or read that specific book, that they may be interested in order for them to function in school.

I would also advise autistic people to try the best that they can in school and to not limit yourself because you have a disability because you can be anything you want to be and much more.

MY IDEAS
FOR MY NEXT BOOKS

- NARCISSISM
- SPECIAL CONNECTIONS TO SPORTS AND MUSIC
- MY EXPERIENCE GROWING UP IN DETROIT
- HOW MY SPECIAL TALENTS WITH DATES HELPS ME WITH EVERYDAY LIFE
- MY AUTISTIC HABITS AND HOW I OVER CAME THEM
- MY SPECIAL CONNECTIONS TO MY SIBLINGS, NIECES, AND NEPHEWS
- MY EXPERIENCES IN THE WORKFORCE
- MY AUTISTIC WITH BULLYING
- DRUG WARS
- THE 2008 RECESSION
- HOW I USED TO GET SICK ON MY BIRTHDAY AND HOW I OVER CAME THAT

www.ingramcontent.com/pod-product-compliance
Lightning Source LLC
Chambersburg PA
CBHW070654050426
42451CB00008B/347